I MARRIED WONDER WOMAN...

NOW WHAT?

I MARRIED WONDER WOMAN...

NOW WHAT?

*A SUPERHERO'S GUIDE
FOR LEADING AND
LOVING THE
PROVERBS 31 WIFE*

JESS MacCALLUM

Standard®
PUBLISHING
Bringing The Word to Life

Cincinnati, Ohio

Published by Standard Publishing, Cincinnati, Ohio
www.standardpub.com

Copyright © 2007 by Jess MacCallum

Project editor: Laura Derico
Cover design: DeAnna Pierce, Bill Chiaravalle—Brand Navigation, LLC
Interior design: Terra Petersen, Bill Chiaravalle—Brand Navigation, LLC

ISBN 978-0-7847-1945-9

13 12 11 10 09 08 07   9 8 7 6 5 4 3 2 1

Library of Congress Cataloging-in-Publication Data
MacCallum, Jess, 1964-
  I married wonder woman-- now what? : a superhero's guide for leading and
loving the Proverbs 31 wife / Jess MacCallum.
     p. cm.
  ISBN 978-0-7847-1945-9 (perfect bound)
  1. Marriage--Religious aspects--Christianity. 2. Sex role--Religious
aspects--Christianity. 3. Bible. O.T. Proverbs XXXI--Criticism,
interpretation, etc. I. Title.

BV835.M185 2007
248.8'425--dc22

2006038954

FROM MR. INCREDIBLE TO MRS. INCREDIBLE:

YOU ARE MY
GREATEST ADVENTURE—
AND I ALMOST MISSED IT.

THE INCREDIBLES, 2005

TABLE OF CONTENTS

INTRODUCTION

PERHAPS YOU'VE SEEN THE LOFTY DESCRIPTION OF THE EXCELLENT WIFE FOUND IN THE SECOND HALF OF PROVERBS 31. It has challenged (and aggravated) women for centuries and given men a sort of checklist for the ideal spouse. A kind of Wonder Woman for her time.

Remember the comic-book heroine Wonder Woman? She was the Amazon Princess Diana who came to defend America against the Nazis in the 1940s, and to do it in a costume less than one-third of what any male superhero wore. Let me tell you, the show created from the comic-book series made for must-see TV in the 1970s, starring Lynda "How-DID-you-get-that-costume-on?" Carter. She played a mild-mannered army secretary to the pearly toothed Major Steve Trevor (Lyle Waggoner from the *Carol Burnett Show*), and cleverly disguised her statuesque good looks with (you guessed it) glasses and a hair bun. But remember, Superman had already proven that people were unobservant dupes who could be fooled by some ten-dollar frames and a little Brylcreem. Never mind that he wore a size 68 jacket, with a 38-inch waist. So why couldn't an Amazon princess hide her six-foot-plus frame, long raven hair, and piercing blue eyes behind a pair of flat-lensed glasses and an olive-drab uniform? (All serious superheroes had raven hair and blue eyes until 1962 when auburn-haired Peter Parker swung into action as Spider-Man.)

Today, *wonder woman* is a euphemism for an active, strong woman in any arena. But the fact is, the comic-book character never took on the really hard stuff; she could only type 120 words a minute and save America—she never tried to manage a household and live a godly life. Wonder Woman 31 from Proverbs truly does it *all*—home management, business development, real estate, culinary arts. She's decisive, analytical, detailed, rational, kind, caring, socially adept, and godly—a wife, mother, employer, business owner. But the comic-book heroine and today's wonder woman do have two big things in common. First, sometimes we pearly toothed hunks can't see past their clever disguises. And second, they rarely get the credit they deserve.

My guess is that, over the centuries, this Proverbs heroine has been unfairly used by some men (me!) as a framework to criticize their spouses—pointing to their shortcomings rather than encouraging their progress. In doing this myself there's something I have come to see behind these verses, even with my own myopic X-ray vision. They subtly reveal a man I was not familiar with—not just a lucky guy who ended up with Supergal. Someone more appropriate for her—someone I wanted to know.

If you haven't ever read about the woman in Proverbs 31, or if it's been a while, read it, and then ask yourself this: What on earth would that kind of woman see in a man like me? And what kind of a superman would I have to become to keep ahead of a wife like this? Obviously, every characteristic that applies to the woman in this passage may not apply to your wife today. Then again, maybe you are blessed with a spouse exactly like her. In any case, we husbands can encourage our wives on their Proverbs 31 journey in the best way possible: by being worthy of them. This is my personal, untrained, didn't-go-to-Bible-college interpretation of what Christ did for his followers: **"For their sakes I sanctify myself" (John 17:19)**. I set myself apart for her benefit, not only my own.

The greatest catalyst for change the Holy Spirit has ever used in my life is my wife. Though she would balk at the pedestal I put her on, she inspires me to be a better man. Like the T-shirt I once read—"I'm their leader. Which way did they go?"—I scramble to lead and encourage the "little (wonder) woman." Far from being intimidated by her, I am eager to give my wonder woman a man she can call her hero.

Throughout the course of this handy guide, I'll pass on twelve indispensable items you're going to need in your utility belt for loving and leading the Proverbs 31 Wonder Woman for a lifetime. If you practice each of these principles, you'll be well equipped for whatever challenge or adventure comes your way. So tighten your cape, and let's swing into action!

AN **EXCELLENT WIFE,**

WHO CAN FIND?

FOR **HER WORTH** IS

FAR ABOVE JEWELS.

PROVERBS 31:10

<table>
<tr><td>UTILITY
BELT
ITEM
#1</td><td>## VALUE YOUR WIFE
ABOVE EVERYTHING</td></tr>
</table>

I MARRIED MY WIFE BECAUSE I COULDN'T IMAGINE EVER FINDING HER EQUAL. I was in love, and I was also impressed. Her value was so clear that there was no way I was going to let her get away if I could do anything about it. I began with the perspective Adam had toward Eve when he first laid eyes on her: *Wow!*

Long red hair, a natural, earthy style, and mischievous brown eyes that said, *If you can't take a joke, you're going to regret ever meeting me.* I certainly didn't know God's will for my life the first time I saw her, but I thought I knew *my* will for my life. As Wayne said of Cassandra in *Wayne's World,* "She will be mine. Oh yes, she will be mine."

Proverbs 18:22 states, "He who finds a wife finds a good thing and obtains favor from the Lord." God's plan is to bless us men through this good thing. I had no doubt that this young lady was a very good thing! And just having her would be favor enough.

I spent time getting to know her while keeping my true identity as Super Smitten Man a secret. I spent a lot of time praying for God's direction and, of course, blabbing to anyone else who'd listen and hopefully mention my fondness to her. It seemed that every time we were around each other, her value to me grew.

In fact, I had seven years to confirm that she was valuable, as she mostly ignored me. Well, *ignored* may be too strong: the thesaurus says *disregarded, overlooked, or bypassed* would be equally descriptive. Just pick one. The point is, I finally caught her. The details of our courtship are relatively unimportant, since every couple has their own story, but eventually, I got her. The compliment of my life was that she traded all her other options (and they were numerous) for me. Like her new title "Mrs.", I felt like I deserved a prefix too—something like "The Amazing," "The Incredible," or "The Fantastic."

A strong beginning like I practiced is not terribly unusual though, and many men proudly show off their catches. Unfortunately however, over time we men often fade in our enthusiasm as other things compete for our attention. Our "good thing" becomes part of the everyday scenery, and values become relative. Not intentionally usually, and not because the good thing has stopped being good in itself. But life is sneaky—you have to watch it every minute or stuff happens. Stuff that makes you go to counseling and sit there with your arms crossed, trying to sound like you're not the one with the problem. Stuff that ends marriages, with each side certain it was the other's fault.

We get distracted rather easily from pursuing our spouse's full potential. It's like investing in a house, expecting it to appreciate, but never spraying for termites, painting, roofing, and doing all the other smart things. Then one day, surprise—you're the one bringing down the neighborhood property values. Sort of like the guy in Luke 14 who started a project he couldn't afford to finish and was ridiculed for poor planning. That scenario is just as possible in our marriages if we stop seeing the value of continuing to invest in our wives.

17

A husband of the Proverbs 31 variety guards against any loss of esteem for his wife. He finds ways to refresh the perspective he had when he first proposed. Not the spark, not the fire, not the chemistry, or any other combustible romantic metaphor, but the value. Value by definition is enduring. And it can be enhanced.

If you think you may have lost a little wonder of your woman, don't panic. But don't just sit there either. The fix is relatively un-mysterious: reevaluate the worth of things according to Scripture and maturity. Now, if you don't at least own a Bible, you will be at a disadvantage here. This is where all transcendent things and all temporal things are categorized and explained. (If your wife knows why you want to read it, I'll bet she'd go out in a blizzard to get you one.)

Once you've looked for a while at what God values, you'll begin to see your own choices differently. All of them.

Sometimes it's a tough lesson to discover that **"what this world honors is an abomination in the sight of God" (Luke 16:15, *NLT*)**. This means some of my personal treasures might need to go. The things that God honors need to show up in my choices.

TOP TEN THINGS
THAT MIGHT SPELL
A SUPERHERO'S UNDOING!
(AND YOURS TOO!)

1. KRYPTONITE (or other crippling substance)

2. SELF-PITY FROM BEING MISUNDERSTOOD

3. INABILITY TO HOLD A STEADY JOB

4. LEADING A DOUBLE LIFE

5. TEMPTING WORKPLACE ROMANCE

6. ASSUMED INVINCIBILITY

7. SHUNNING TEAMWORK

8. A PARTICULAR FEMALE VILLAIN

9. ANGER OR FRUSTRATION OVER INNER TURMOIL

10. BITTERNESS FROM LACK OF APPRECIATION

So if the value Christ placed on the church is any indication of how a husband is to see his wife (Ephesians 5:25), then clearly the things that compete for my wife's rightful spot should be dealt with ruthlessly and heroically.

Scripture is, of course, the foundation for truth and value, but after that comes just plain growing up. Maturity brings a different perspective and changes what we value for the better. Unfortunately, age doesn't equal maturity. There are way too many fifteen-year-old souls running around in fifty-year-old bodies. And I know this comes as a shocker, but even having the Holy Spirit isn't a guarantee of mature thinking, or else we wouldn't know so many Christians we'd never invite to dinner. Maturity, as far as I can tell, is a series of decisions over time. Some we make under outside pressure. ("Happy birthday, son! You're twenty-six today. Please move out.") Some we make because a lightbulb goes off in our heads. ("If Dad isn't going to raise my allowance to $450 a week, I guess I need a job.") But decision making and taking responsibility for our actions is the formula for maturity, no matter the stimulus. Remember what Uncle Ben told Peter Parker? "With great power comes great responsibility." And he didn't even know Peter was Spider-Man! He was just talking about growing up. We as men have been given great power. We forget this only because it sometimes lies untapped beneath a big pile of potential.

The good news is that your wife is just waiting to respond; the far-above-jewels woman in her will come out all the more. Interesting isn't it, the comparison is to jewels, since they are most valuable in their final, polished form? What a foolish thing to ignore the value of a diamond, even if it's still in the rough!

> **THE PROVERBS 31 HUSBAND GETS HIS VALUES IN ORDER AND MAKES SURE HE GUARDS HIS MOST VALUABLE TREASURE.**

THE **HEART** OF HER **HUSBAND**
TRUSTS IN HER,
AND HE WILL **HAVE NO LACK** OF GAIN.
SHE **DOES HIM GOOD** AND NOT **EVIL**
ALL THE DAYS OF HER **LIFE.**

PROVERBS 31:11, 12

TRUST YOUR WIFE
AND REAP
THE BENEFITS

ON OUR HONEYMOON WE RENTED A TWO-SEATER BICYCLE. My wife, Anne, wanted to steer first, so I took the camera and provided pedal power. It was a little funny trying to get our balance, and I had to get used to a handlebar that didn't move. (If you've never ridden on the back of a two-seater, imagine being on a stationary bike at the gym but with the possibility that someone might push you over and make you skin your knee.) But after half a mile or so, I was engrossed in picture taking, pedaling without holding on. We were laughing and talking like— well, like newlyweds.

When we finally decided to head back, there was a slight problem. We had agreed to switch at this point, and she had a hard time not being in control. After only a few seconds of pedaling from the back and realizing that her handlebars were welded in place, she yelled, "How did you do this?! This is freaking me out!"

"It's a trust thing, isn't it?" I called back to her as she tugged at the immobile bar—she might as well have been trying to steer a station wagon by the bumper. "Takes a little getting used to, doesn't it?" I said smugly.

"I don't want to be back here long enough to get used to it!" she yelled.

We made it back OK. What started as a romantic ride had become a small, intimate adventure. I had inadvertently leaped a tall building in a single bound, awing her with my relaxed trust in her steering. And boy, did I reap the benefits, scoring big points with my new wife. Not a bad idea on your honeymoon.

It was a little thing, but it has served as a metaphor for us ever since. Over the years she has proven herself more and more trustworthy (as I hope I have) in the larger areas of our lives. I have certainly benefited from this.

HERE'S A LITTLE QUIZ
ON **TRUSTING** YOUR **WIFE**

1. DO YOU LET HER PICK OUT YOUR CLOTHES FOR IMPORTANT EVENTS? (5 points)

2. CAN YOU LET HER DRIVE FOR MORE THAN FIFTEEN MINUTES WITHOUT COMMENT? (10 points)

3. DOES YOUR WIFE BALANCE THE CHECKING ACCOUNT? (102 points)

4. ARE YOU CURRENTLY WEARING YOUR HAIR/BEARD IN A STYLE SHE CHOSE? (15 points)

5. HAVE YOU EVER PASSED OFF ONE OF HER SUGGESTIONS AS YOUR OWN AT WORK? (50 points)

6. IN AN ALL-MALE GATHERING, HAVE YOU EVER UTTERED THE PHRASE "MY WIFE HAD A GREAT IDEA LAST NIGHT"? (200 points)

7. HAVE YOU EVER HAD SEX WITHOUT CONTRACEPTION BECAUSE SHE SAID, "IT'S OK, I WON'T GET PREGNANT"? (8124 points)

If you scored above **8000** on this quiz, you are the **Man of Steel.**

But I must admit, as the stakes have risen higher than a skinned knee from a wrecked two-seater, I have not always been able to relax in my trust so easily. This is the tricky part in the verse—trust from the heart. It's not far off what we read in **Proverbs 3:5, "Trust in the Lord with all your heart."** (Of course, the obvious difference is that the Lord is perfect and my wife is not, but the source of trust is still *my* heart.)

I recently was challenged by the attitude of a guy who isn't even a Christian. In an address called "Women Waging Peace," given on November 13, 2003, by one of the few women invited to be on Iraq's Interim Governing Council, Dr. Rajaa Habib Dhahir Khuzai described her process for deciding to accept the position: "I said I would have to think about it, so I went home and discussed it with my family and husband. I had the full encouragement and support of my husband. He said that after helping so many women give birth to Iraqi babies, it was time to help give birth to a new Iraqi society." Does this husband have some kind of confidence in his wife or what? Enough at least to risk reprisals, death threats, and living in a society she gets to help build. What a challenge to Christian husbands!

Begrudging my trust is largely my own issue. My wife certainly has an outstanding track record of trustworthiness. This reminds me of the Spider-Man comics I read religiously as a kid. For some reason he was always viewed with a little suspicion even after he saved the city over and over. What was wrong with those people anyway? In fact, the mistrusted do-gooder is not an uncommon character in superhero lore. In the animated movie *The Incredibles,* a family of superheroes has to enter a protection and relocation program after society has rejected people with superpowers. People don't trust them because they are different, and their methods of dealing with things can be dramatic. And isn't that the only excuse I have left for not wholeheartedly trusting my own wonder wife? That she might do things dramatically different than I would? Has she really not done enough for me to trust her from the heart? Maybe I should stop being like the crusty newspaper editors waiting for the mighty heroes to fall, and more like a grateful passenger whose train was just rescued from disaster by a gal in a star-spangled, spandex one-piece and some go-go boots!

So what if she doesn't deflect every bullet with her magic wristbands? (If you're not familiar with the Wonder Woman

27

character, then you should know that she had these really cool indestructible bracers, and she was so fast she could deflect bullets! No really, I saw her do it every week from 1975 to 1979.) And what if once in a while she doesn't arrive in the nick of time? Even if you get handed a disappointment now and then, it's still better to live your life trusting your mate than to do the alternative. The apostle Paul knew this when he said **"love always trusts" (1 Corinthians 13)**. We are better off choosing love and trust over fearfulness and suspicion. What I stand to gain from trusting my superwife in this life is reason enough to trust her, even with some mishaps.

Besides, would we amazing guys really stand up to the same kind of assessment we give our wives? Not me! Do you realize how often I've forgotten to wear my cape under my suit? how many times the Bat-Signal has gone unanswered? how often I've slept through the attack of the giant mechanized battle-rabbits of doom? Surely I can give my Wonder Woman 31 a couple of chances.

One last thought. Notice the length of time referenced in Proverbs 31:12. The perspective is one that looks back over a lifetime. All of us have grown up in a generation when most of our wants or needs are gratified quickly, like the Flash at a Chinese buffet. But God built the seed principle into trusting our wives. You know that principle: With time, something grand comes out of something small; with time, something unimaginable comes from something plain. I know my wife responds to the confidence I place in her, and I get the "no lack of gain" part found in verse 11. Nobody in his right mind makes an intentionally bad investment. Risky maybe, but bad, never. And the investment we make in our wives, however risky it might feel, deserves the time it requires to benefit us both.

> **THE PROVERBS 31 HUSBAND UNDERSTANDS THE RETURN ON HIS INVESTMENT OF TRUST. EVEN IN THE FACE OF RISK, HE PLACES HIS FULL TRUST IN HIS HEROINE.**

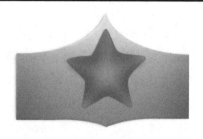

SHE **LOOKS** FOR **WOOL** AND **FLAX**
AND **WORKS** WITH HER HANDS
IN DELIGHT.
SHE IS LIKE **MERCHANT SHIPS;**
SHE **BRINGS** HER **FOOD** FROM AFAR.
SHE RISES ALSO WHILE IT IS
STILL **NIGHT**
AND **GIVES FOOD** TO HER **HOUSEHOLD**
AND **PORTIONS** TO HER **MAIDENS.**

PROVERBS 31:13-15

<table>
<tr><td>UTILITY
BELT
ITEM
◆#3◆</td><td># PROVIDE FOR THE FAMILY WITH MORE THAN MONEY</td></tr>
</table>

IN MY DAD'S DAY (THINK THE DEPRESSION, WWII, AND BERMUDA SHORTS WITH BLACK SOCKS), THE MAN WAS THE PROVIDER, THE BREADWINNER. And that pretty much gave him the right every night to put on his slippers, light his pipe, and eat a TV dinner while watching the *CBS Evening News* with Walter Cronkite. In other words, he provided an income, some basic lawn care, and was then free to do whatever he pleased. And to be fair to my dad (and all the other John Wayne types), many women found that arrangement perfectly acceptable, including my own mother. In fact, she once told me that Dad's work ethic was one of the things that she found attractive in him. Who says accounting isn't a sexy career?

In Proverbs 31:13-15, this competent and capable woman appears to be taking care of things without her husband's involvement, except for maybe some behind-the-scenes work on his part of supplying the finances. Clearly she's got the resources to take care of the entire household, including some helpers. She's a real go-getter, maybe even a Type A personality.

But one day, as I was mowing the lawn in Bermuda shorts and black socks, I wondered: Was the fact that her husband was bringing home a paycheck enough to cause this woman, like my own mother, like my own wife, to work "in delight" (also translated "willingly")?

Was my wife getting up early, making an extra effort in so many areas simply because she knew I was gainfully employed? I knew of families with far fewer resources whose wives showed the same kind of Wonder Woman 31 attitude, enthusiastically taking care of their households. (Conversely, I had seen well-heeled women who were very busy, but like a woman under a load rather than on top of her game.) **What was the husband in Proverbs 31 providing beyond finances that enabled her in turn to provide like she did "in delight"?**

STAYING CONNECTED TO GOD

1. CREATE A SECRET SANCTUM. It doesn't matter where it is, so long as it gives you daily uninterrupted time with God. No hero can be super for long without such a place.

2. ESTABLISH A LEAGUE OF EXTRAORDINARY GENTLEMEN. Sharing common goals and struggles with a team of peers who can relate will inspire you.

3. RESCUE THE WEAK. For a season, pledge to serve the neediest people you can find: toddlers, prisoners, the elderly, the homeless. It will drive you to God.

4. RECRUIT A SIDEKICK. Mentoring requires sacrifice and devotion, but insures that men with potential become superheroes themselves. Even Superman was Superboy once.

5. SAVE THE WORLD. Research and pray for specific countries, continents, and missionaries for one hour a month with your wonder woman and the kids.

6. TAKE THE PLEDGE. Upholding justice is good, but pursuing holiness is better. Pledge to make private sacrifices to God. Commit to fasting regularly, forsaking lingering bad habits, memorizing Scripture—anything that will stretch you but that only God can see.

Did he, or my dad for that matter, have a secret that energized his fantastic spouse? Could providing a larger sense of security have been the thing that kept her going willingly rather than in drudgery? Was it—and I hate to sound like Captain Whipped—emotional support too?

Now, I am a big believer in a man providing financially for his family. Maybe it's because I was raised by a WWII vet. Maybe it's because I was raised by an accountant. Both, I suspect. But I have also had unique spiritual experiences in seeking God's provision for my family. When I quit my job as an artist to work as a salesman for a printing company, I did it for the money. We were expecting our first child, and we both wanted my wife to be at home full-time. She kept up with a flexible part-time job, while I worked two jobs: sales in the day and freelance graphic design at night. During the early years of my career, I learned clearly how "give us this day our daily bread" worked. What I sold one day worked its way onto our dinner table in about thirty-five to forty days, when I received my commission check. My payment for my freelance art took a little longer to collect and often required physical threats. The whole experience stretched me so far I felt like Dr. Reed Richards—Mr. Fantastic of the Fantastic Four.

But far beyond wage earning—your wife might even earn more than you—husbands are designed to be spiritual and emotional providers. That is what I want to stress here. For most women, security is not just financial. Money is, of course, a factor. But as usual, women look at a bigger picture (which is why, unlike many men, they will marry for reasons other than looks). But providing that big-picture sense of security for her can be tough; it's ambiguous, takes time, can't easily be monitored, and worst of all, it means planning. Remember the Riddler on the old *Batman* TV series? Well, riddle me this, Caped Crusader: What two root words are found in the word *provision? **Pro*—ahead or before; and *vision*—seeing or insight.**

Incidentally, if any of those evil masterminds had ever repented and settled down, they probably would have made great husbands. I mean, all those guys *did* was plan ahead—poisoning the water supply to blackmail the East Coast; brainwashing Nobel Prize winners to deploy particle beam weapons over day-care centers; cloning Jimmy Carter for another go at the White House—that's a lot of work! Imagine if they had turned that kind of energy toward making a marriage work!

Taking the time to analyze and look ahead, to project and weigh, then commit to a course of action isn't my superpower. I like to shoot from the hip. It makes me tired just thinking about thinking ahead. (This is the source of the Friday-night-romance-killing phrase, "I dunno, hun, whatta *you* wanna do?") But the security of banks, businesses, or nations—and marriages—depends on planning ahead. Thankfully, like the helpless citizens of Metropolis, we husbands have hope. I'll give you a hint where to start: "Look, up in the sky!"

When Hollywood rediscovered comic-book themes, its first big-budget movie was *Superman,* in 1978, starring the late Christopher Reeve. The movie's tagline was "You'll believe a man can fly!" which apparently had been the big holdup in making this before 1978. But thanks to some cutting-edge camera work (blue screens and the Zoptics technique), you could hardly see the wires! (Digital retouching on computers was still a long way off—it's hard to create a CGI script on an Apple II with a whopping 12K RAM). So of course, flying scenes were all over this movie. After Clark Kent lands a job at the *Daily Planet,* his first big rescue involves a news helicopter and reporter Lois Lane. As she's falling to an unquestionably messy death, he swoops in and catches her! Though she is shocked to meet someone on her way to the pavement, Superman calmly reassures her, "Easy, miss. I've got you." She looks around and stammers back, "You—You've got *me*?! Who's got *you*?!"

That's a really valid question for women, if you think about it. What keeps us men from hitting the ground? Women really want to know where the wires go. In Lois Lane's paradigm, what holds *him* up translates to what holds *her* up. For our wives, the larger picture of spiritual and emotional support includes our own connection to God. How I stay aloft spiritually could mean, for her, the difference between clouds and pavement. In Superman's case, his support is merely superhuman. In the case of a Proverbs 31 husband, it's supernatural.

Our dear wonder wives need to be sure that we are connected to God as we fly around with them in our arms. Since the root of all real security comes from God, if I am *actively* tied to him, my wife will "believe a man can fly"! (Later in the movie, when Superman and Lois fly again, Lois has a totally different experience—exhilaration!) If I don't hang my wires to Christ, I might as well trade my red cape and matching boots for those

Bermuda shorts and black socks, 'cause I ain't getting off the ground. For my Wonder Woman 31 to soar with delight, I have to provide for her in every way I can think of. And don't think security doesn't play a direct role in the bedroom! If you start working on creating a more secure environment for her, you are going to really feel, well . . . super!

THE PROVERBS 31 HUSBAND REALIZES THAT HIS WIFE NEEDS SECURITY, AND THAT SECURITY STARTS WITH HIS OWN CONNECTION TO GOD.

SHE **CONSIDERS** A FIELD AND **BUYS** IT;

FROM HER **EARNINGS**

SHE PLANTS A VINEYARD. . . .

SHE MAKES **LINEN GARMENTS**

AND **SELLS THEM,**

AND **SUPPLIES BELTS** TO THE

TRADESMEN.

PROVERBS 31:16, 24

DON'T BE AFRAID OF HER INDEPENDENCE OR INTIMIDATED BY HER SUCCESS

THERE IS AN INVISIBLE STRING TIED FROM MY HEART TO MY WALLET. ACTUALLY IT'S MORE LIKE A REALLY THICK WIRE. OK . . . it's a braided steel cable. It's hard enough for me to take risks with money myself, much less watch my wife do it.

Picture this scene: you come home from a business trip and ask, "Anything interesting happen while I was away?"

And she says, "Yes! I bought something I've been thinking about for some time."

"Oh," you respond casually, "clothes? shoes? furniture?"

"No. Thirty-two acres near the river. And next week the workers are coming."

If I came home and my wife announced she had invested in real estate and begun her own vineyard, I would probably need some wine right then and there. (Maybe it wouldn't be a problem if her maiden name was Gallo or Mondavi, but it isn't.) Risk-taking has just never been part of my natural makeup; I learned it slowly in the marketplace.

The fact is, I didn't expect to be in business. I was an art major! I wanted to be a cartoonist or an illustrator or in some similar long-haired, unshaven occupation. I even thought we might be on the mission field one day—anything but business. Now I am a partner in a large commercial printing company. God's direction still puzzles me sometimes. The marketplace is part crucible, part backyard football, and part grad school. But only there could I have learned certain lessons of faith and character. (I should quickly point out that that includes lessons on *lack* of faith and *deficits* in character.) In a business environment, no greater area gets addressed than decision making. The analysis, the risk, and the immediate consequences drive me toward God.

I am required to develop leadership, patience, good judgment, intuition, and vision. In other words, I have to grow up or explode in front of witnesses.

Who wouldn't want that for his wife too? (The growing up part, I mean.) Who wouldn't benefit from a wife who grew in these critical character areas? They translate to every aspect of life, from church to children, from the boardroom to the bedroom. **Jesus says the way we handle "unrighteous wealth"—worldly stuff—is a testing ground before being allowed to become a steward of "true riches"—spiritual stuff (Luke 16:11).** Better you learn to soar by jumping off the garage with a towel for a cape than to step off the top floor of the *Daily Planet* where Jimmy, Lois, and Perry can laugh as you bounce off the pavement and make front-page headlines.

Clearly, failure in business can carry some heavy consequences, but it is preferable to take risks and learn how to use *play* money in the eyes of God before we have eternal consequences. The husband suited to lead Wonder Woman 31 may have to exercise nerves of steel as he supports his wife in the face of financial risk. Even if you or your wife has no interest in business, the

43

GET USED TO
WOMEN IN BUSINESS

According to the Center for Women's Business Research:

- AS OF 2004 THERE WERE AN ESTIMATED 10.6 MILLION PRIVATELY OWNED BUSINESSES WHERE WOMEN OWNED 50 PERCENT OR MORE OF THE COMPANY. THAT'S NEARLY HALF (47.7 percent) OF *ALL* PRIVATELY HELD COMPANIES.

- THESE BUSINESSES GENERATED AN ESTIMATED $2.46 TRILLION IN SALES AND EMPLOYED 19.1 MILLION PEOPLE.

- BETWEEN 1997 AND 2004, THE GROWTH OF THIS TYPE OF BUSINESS WAS NEARLY *TWICE* THE RATE OF ALL PRIVATE FIRMS.

principle still applies to her personal development: allow her the independence to make important decisions.

Of course, there's the flip side of this coin. What if your wife is a whole lot better at this than you are? What if she's just naturally smarter in business (or in making critical decisions) than you? What if you're the one clipping recipes from *Ladies' Home Journal* and she's reading the *Wall Street Journal?* What if she can leap a taller building in a single bound?! Maybe your wife was established in a career or was already a success in business before you got married. Then you probably knew what you were in for . . . sort of. I confess I am glad I don't compete against my wife in business. She's pretty shrewd. Maybe a star businesswoman in the family would be a dream come true. But maybe some of us would be intimidated by a little competition. If we were brutally honest with ourselves, maybe we would admit that her success would seem worse to us than her failure.

The only real obstacle to being thrilled by our wives' greater success is, of course, our male egos. That's why every major sitcom uses this gimmick; shows like *Tool Time, Everybody Loves Raymond,* and *King of Queens* have built entire seasons off watching competitive husbands get bested by their wives. But nothing takes the intimidated husband theme to the heights of the 2004 comic remake, *The Stepford Wives.* In an exclusive suburb in Connecticut, the husbands dealt with their high-powered spouses, and their own inferiority complexes, by having computer chips implanted in the women's heads, transforming them into "ideal" wives. Of course, they programmed them to look and act like sexy Betty Crockers, who could also caddy.

Our natural competitiveness may get out of whack and be misdirected toward our spouses. It doesn't mean you aren't leading if your wife makes more money or garners more recognition (unless, of course, you quit leading because of it). Leadership in the home always falls to the husband to initiate. No matter what the outside world rewards or praises, God is the one who assigned husbands their role, and if he gave you a wonder (business) woman, then enjoy the ride.

THE PROVERBS 31 HUSBAND HAS A BALANCED VIEW OF HIS WIFE. HE SUPPORTS HER RISK TAKING AND DELIGHTS IN HER SUCCESSES.

SHE **GIRDS** HERSELF WITH **STRENGTH**
AND MAKES HER **ARMS STRONG.**
SHE **SENSES** THAT HER **GAIN** IS **GOOD;**
HER LAMP DOES NOT GO OUT
AT **NIGHT.**
SHE **STRETCHES** OUT HER **HANDS**
TO THE **DISTAFF,**
AND HER HANDS GRASP THE SPINDLE.

PROVERBS 31:17-19

<table>
<tr><td>UTILITY
BELT
ITEM
⟨#5⟩</td><td>## APPRECIATE HER INTELLIGENCE, AMBITION, AND DRIVE</td></tr>
</table>

MY FATHER ONCE PAID MY MOTHER THE GREATEST 1950s COMPLIMENT. "Honey," he said, "you think like a man." What he was saying, of course, was that she impressed him with her ambition and personal drive. Before they were married, Mom worked for the local television station and had her own midday show (in Wilmington, North Carolina, 1959). She was a single parent breaking into a new industry in a small Southern town. She began by modeling for the local newspaper when stores wanted to show the season's new fashions, and by reading radio weather reports during her lunch break—both for free! She even bought a reel-to-reel tape player to practice her speaking voice and to refine her country accent.

The hurdles she faced and the superhuman efforts she made were not lost on my dad. He knew what leaping a tall building looked like—even in Wilmington, North Carolina, in 1959, when the tallest building was maybe four stories high. (It didn't hurt either that she had raven hair, piercing blue eyes, and worked as a secretary—honest!) Her hard work had paid off, and he admired her tenacity and practicality. And even more so when she left it all to marry him and move to a new city. What a compliment that was! And he appreciated it because he knew she would bring that spirit to their marriage. He wasn't disappointed.

I personally do not know a wife who doesn't work hard. And I'm sure no wife with kids would say she has it easy. And let's face it—even in an age where women have equal access to the marketplace, they still seem to get more than equal access to the household chores. As the old adage goes, **"A man may work from sun to sun, but a woman's work is never done."** That's true probably because women are less likely to be quitters. I know if I were to switch places with my wife, I'd close the household down about the time the news came on, and wouldn't reopen it until the automatic coffeemaker had produced its magic elixir the next morning.

My own wife is very ambitious, and I find that . . . challenging. If she really could pick any superhero to be like, she'd choose the Flash, because she's always dashing from one thing to the next. If idle hands are the devil's workshop, then in her case he'll have to find a new place to tinker. She is perpetually involved in projects at home and events elsewhere; there seems no end of people she's encouraging, music she's writing and recording, or books she's reading. And in her spare time there are three kids she's homeschooling. She hates to waste time; consequently, she never watches TV. She works when she's sick and is always in motion.

I fear to think what I would be like without this in-house stimulus. I tend toward couches and movies more than is healthy. (If I hadn't hitched up with her, the closest thing to exercise I'd get is searching for the remote in the sofa cushions between commercials.) But keeping up with this kind of woman has not only given me a physical workout, she's helped me get in shape mentally and spiritually too. As Peter Parker says in the movie *Spider-Man,* describing the effect M. J., his one true love, has on him: "You don't know what you feel, you just know what kind of man you want to be."

I have come to enjoy the rarefied atmosphere my wife creates. I am doing things far beyond my natural bent, outside my comfort zone, and sometimes without a safety net. She is directly responsible for my being a business owner, renovating my own house, taking up gourmet cooking, and writing this book. (Some days, I admit, it's like having high-altitude cerebral edema. I have to catch my breath frequently, or pass out and be carried down to safety by a Saint Bernard.)

There is a guy in my church who has set the standard for me by the way he supported his talented, ambitious wife. For a couple of years, I had seen her working with the children's ministry, but that was about all I knew of her. When I mentioned to my wife that I would like to have a current family portrait for my office, she told me this young lady was a photographer. So we made an appointment for a family sitting. Truthfully, I really didn't know what to expect, since she works in a studio at her house. I figured it was worth a try and maybe we'd get a few good shots.

When she showed us the proofs, I was blown away. She was outstanding—every single shot was amazing. No contorted poses, no glare off my bald head, no closed eyes. Nothing had prepared me for such fantastic results. No wonder her husband supported her foray into photography. But here's the real wonder of it all—and I can hardly bring myself to write these words—her studio is their single-car garage. THE MAN GAVE UP HIS GARAGE! I mean there was *nothing* in it but her equipment. He piled everything a garage is supposed to have into a shed in the backyard. When I asked him how he could do something so diametrically opposed to millennia of evolution, he just shrugged and said, "She's really good." That is a man who appreciates his wife's ambition and talents.

THE PROVERBS 31 HUSBAND SHOWS HIS WIFE HOW MUCH HE APPRECIATES HER MOTIVATION AND ENCOURAGES HER AS MUCH AS POSSIBLE.

TONS OF INITIATIVE

SHORTLY AFTER WE MOVED INTO OUR CURRENT HOUSE ABOUT EIGHT YEARS AGO, MY WIFE DECIDED TO LANDSCAPE BASICALLY EVERYTHING. The first big hurdle was getting topsoil to create raised beds. Being on a limited budget didn't slow her down. She called a church member who owned a large landscaping company to find out where the cheapest topsoil was. He told her where to get it, but there was one hitch: she'd have to pick it up—three tons of it! I got a phone call later that went something like this:

WONDER WOMAN: Hey, honey, I got the topsoil we needed really cheap! And no delivery charge!

SUPER SUSPICIOUS MAN: Great. When are they going to deliver it?

WONDER WOMAN (with note of pride in voice): Well, actually I got it myself. I'm on the way to the house now.

SUPER SUSPICIOUS MAN: What do mean *you've* got it?? I thought you needed tons of it.

WONDER WOMAN: Well, yeah, I've got about three tons. I borrowed a dump truck.

SUPER SUSPICIOUS MAN: You're driving a dump truck?! Where are the kids? I thought you had to pick Kyle up from school. *(Kyle, our oldest, was a first-grader at the time.)*

WONDER WOMAN: I did pick him up. Baby's at your mom's. Kyle and Anna Claire are in the cab with me. *(Anna Claire was then five.)*

SUPER SUSPICIOUS MAN: You went through the carpool line *in a dump truck?*

WONDER WOMAN: Yeah, Kyle thought it was great! All his friends were watching. The teacher had to lift him up to get in.

SUPER SUSPICIOUS MAN: I suppose the guy who loaned you this truck showed you how to dump it.

WONDER WOMAN: Yeah, it's not that hard. I thought I'd just back it right up in the yard and dump a couple of piles where I needed it.

SUPER SUSPICIOUS MAN: Well, do me a favor. Could you just drop it all in the driveway? I'll move it later with the wheelbarrow.

WONDER WOMAN: Why would you want to do all that extra work?!

SUPER SUSPICIOUS MAN: Because I'm guessing that between the dirt and the truck, you've got well over ten tons and I don't want to call the city to come and fix a broken water line. OK?

WONDER WOMAN: Hey, that's a good thought! I'm glad I called.

SUPER SUSPICIOUS MAN: Yeah, me too.

SHE **EXTENDS** HER **HAND**
TO THE POOR,
AND **SHE** STRETCHES OUT **HER**
HANDS TO THE NEEDY.

PROVERBS 31:20

<table>
<tr><td>

UTILITY

BELT

ITEM

#6

</td><td>

BE UNSELFISH LIKE HER AND WITH HER

</td></tr>
</table>

WE ARE ALL SOMETHING OF A BLEND OF OUR PARENTS (DUH). In the 2005 movie *Sky High,* the world's greatest hero, The Commander, and his wife, Jetstream, have a son who inherits both their superpowers: superstrength and superspeed. In *The Incredibles,* the kids all get different powers from their parents, but they are all "supers." In my case I generally have all my mother's strengths and most of my father's weaknesses. So that means I genuinely care about my fellow man, unless I am driving; I am a compassionate listener, until you say something stupid; and I am spontaneously generous, but get really angry later when I try to balance the checkbook. My Catholic mother taught me that by sharing with the poor, we honor God, and my Presbyterian father taught me that giving a tenth of our income was required—and we should be thankful God never raised the percentage like the federal government does.

So inside rages this epic battle between faith and fear when it comes to people and giving. And I'm going to be as transparent about this as Sue Storm, the Invisible Girl from the Fantastic Four—I really don't feel comfortable with the category called "the poor." For some time I have been trying to see past the political volleyball this group has become and gain a biblical, yet contemporary, view. For example, earlier in Proverbs, this attitude is described: **"Those who oppress the poor insult their Maker, but helping the poor honors him" (14:31, _NLT_)**. And in another part, "Those who mock the poor insult their Maker; those who rejoice at the misfortune of others will be punished" (17:5, _NLT_). It is significant that the poor and the unfortunate are both tied directly to God himself. But I have a hard time seeing this connection.

While I labor to formulate a definition in my own mind as to who "the poor" are, one thing is beyond evading—I haven't gotten close to any of the people who might qualify. Sure, I give the money, but it's from a safe distance. Envision the Green Lantern guiding a crippled airliner to a safe landing with the emerald beam from his Zsa Zsa Gabor-sized ring—waving good-bye to all the grateful passengers as he speeds away to an Irish pub where people in green blend in. Never actually getting his hands dirty (the ring did all the work)—securely distant. No first names, no reception, no piggyback rides for the kids. This is me.

By contrast, consider the Proverbs 31 Wonder Woman. She reaches out *her own hands* to these people. For her, relationships play a key factor in the total scheme of giving. Wonder Woman 31 is close enough to touch and actually engage the needy as (Gasp!) *people,* and does not think herself above doing so. These people to her are not a target or project. She is personal in her sacrifice and sees sharing as natural. Of course, it's no accident that 31:20 follows issues related to business, profit, and hard work. She has produced a return by her labors, and it follows that she is sharing her return.

My wife is like this far more than is comfortable for me. So I have made a conscious choice. This is where I have decided to be a sidekick, like Robin, the Boy Wonder. I can run alongside as she breaks down walls of economic and social separation. I can carry the box of mercy to the unwed mother she is comforting. I can

BITTERNESS CHECKLIST
YOU MIGHT BE TURNING
INTO A VILLAIN IF . . .

- YOU FIND YOURSELF SOLILOQUIZING ABOUT YOUR WIFE'S DOOM.

- YOU START USING PET NAMES LIKE WONDER-WHAT-TOOK-YOU-SO-LONG WOMAN.

- YOU BEGIN PLOTTING TO DOMINATE THE WORLD, STARTING WITH YOUR WIFE WHEN SHE GETS HOME.

- HER NEW NICKNAME FOR YOU IN BED IS THE DEMANDER.

- YOUR FAVORITE SUPERPOWER IS SPITTING POISON WORDS.

- YOU CONSTANTLY SIDE WITH HER NEMESIS, HYPERCRITICAL (*your* mother).

- YOU START DAYDREAMING ABOUT HAVING A HENCH*WOMAN*.

- YOU EVER PULL OUT THE ULTIMATE WEAPON—THE *D* WORD (DIVORCE).

drive the gift-mobile to take her to the downtrodden. And even if I never get that same thrill she does from looking someone in the eye when I give, I can at least follow her lead as she swings into action and shout "Holy itemized deduction!"

But there's one other challenge implied here that the husband of this biblical superwoman faces. More difficult than getting out of his comfort zone, harder than turning money loose—even into the 11 or 12 percent range—is sacrificing the attention and time of his wife. Giving up the greatest woman on earth even for a few evenings a week can be an annoying challenge.

It's a common problem for superheroes too, you know—being torn between the hero work and normal life. Heroes are always on call. More than obstetricians. More than plumbers. More than eBay's tech support. Superheroes *never* get a break. Take Iron Man, for example. How's he supposed to know Dr. Doom is about to attempt planetary dominance while he's trying to unbolt his potty flap? Spider-Man went through it all the time. Try dealing with normal teenage hormones *and* radioactive arthropod DNA, while the Chameleon impersonates your prom date's father. Bruce Wayne was always standing up a young socialite at the opera because the Penguin, who couldn't get a date, never seemed to time his schemes to conform to normal business hours. And Superman . . . well, he just about gave up on the whole relationship thing by retreating to his Fortress of Solitude. (All I have is an unheated tool shed.) And while the torn superheroes got all the sympathy, the would-be significant others got only a line or two to fume about taking a backseat to the "greater good."

Similarly, I have had to wait patiently at home on several occasions while my amazing wife did amazing things for others. Whether it's the needy in the sense of the poor, or just people with pressing needs, my talented wife is in demand; and that leaves me with a choice. Support her like a good sidekick or waste an evening, possibly a whole weekend, being sour. It seems very macho at the time, but on the maturity scale it's only one step above holding my breath till I turn blue. I know my archenemy wants me to believe that I am getting shortchanged while she meets the needs of everyone else. But this is where you and I have the opportunity to strap on our own capes and fight the good fight. We can battle the accusations of the archenemy and share our wives like the heroes they think we are. Thus we live out the command of Paul, **"Husbands, love your wives and do not be embittered against them" (Colossians 3:19).** Being embittered is just as easy toward a great wife as a lousy one, since bitterness starts with disappointment. Unchecked, disappointment grows into resentment, and then takes root as a full-blown attitude problem with squatter's rights.

OK, I think you can plainly see that rescuing the helpless or needy is more exciting to me in theory than in reality. I am a card-carrying member of the O-ye-of-little-faith club when it comes to turning loose my resources, especially my wife. But I can be a good sidekick at least; and with the help of my wonder woman, I will improve. You have my pledge, citizens.

> **THE PROVERBS 31 HUSBAND IS PROUD WHEN HIS WIFE DEMONSTRATES CONCERN, GENEROSITY, AND EMPATHY. THIS IS NOT A THREAT TO HIS NEEDS, AN INCONVENIENCE TO HIS ROUTINE, OR AN UNNECESSARY EXPENSE.**

SHE IS NOT **AFRAID** OF THE **SNOW**
FOR HER HOUSEHOLD,
FOR **ALL** HER **HOUSEHOLD** ARE
CLOTHED WITH SCARLET.
SHE MAKES **COVERINGS** FOR HERSELF;
HER CLOTHING IS
FINE LINEN AND **PURPLE.** . . . .
SHE LOOKS WELL TO THE
WAYS OF **HER HOUSEHOLD,**
AND DOES NOT EAT THE BREAD OF IDLENESS.

PROVERBS 31:21, 22, 27

UTILITY BELT ITEM #7

RESPECT YOUR WIFE'S HOUSEHOLD MANAGEMENT WITHOUT MEDDLING

EVERY MAN'S BRAIN HAS TWO HEMISPHERES. One is the "I don't want to do it myself" side, and the other is the "I would have done it differently if you'd asked me" side. For example, one Friday my wife called me at work to say she had mowed the lawn since it was a beautiful day. *Great!* I thought, *I'm rescued! Now that really frees up my Saturday. Sure hope it looks OK . . . hope she got that strip between us and crusty old man Lambert or I'll hear about it . . . wonder if she just ran over all those pinecones . . .* Why wasn't I just happy to have it checked off my list? Because I have those two sides of the male brain. I don't want another responsibility, but I could have done it better. That's poison for my marriage: delegation accompanied by criticism.

In these verses, Wonder Woman 31 is an outstanding example of diligence, household management, and domestic support. A Martha Stewart in a cape and tights—no, wait, scratch that visual. A lean, mean, homemaking machine. I realize many families no longer fit the profile of my parents' generation—June Cleaver at home, Ward at the office. (What did the Beaver's dad do, anyway?) But this has been the lay of the land for much of my marriage, and I can tell you from sore experience that you should NOT communicate in any way, shape, or form that although she's responsible for managing the homestead, you could do better. At least, not if sex is in your plans this year. **Do NOT imply that mere mortals could do her job.** Do NOT touch her magic lasso! Being a domestic goddess ain't as easy as it looks.

There was a great movie in 1983 that really helped launch Michael Keaton's career—*Mr. Mom.* (If you've never heard of Michael Keaton, then you're probably reading this book by accident and should put it back where your dad can find it.) In the movie, he loses his job at an auto plant, and his wife goes back to work. He stays home to take care of the house and the kids. But he gets stuck there for months because this was the early 1980s and Japan was kicking our butts in the auto industry.

Historical footnote: In 1986, Michael Keaton starred in *Gung Ho*, a movie about a Japanese automaker trying to set up shop in the U.S. The Japanese were able to get a foothold here because people like me would drive used Toyotas or Hondas rather than a new American car built in the early '80s. Not to mention that the '80s were a particularly forgettable period for American auto design. Remember the Chevy Citation, Dodge Aries, Plymouth Reliant K? They looked like pine-box derby cars that somebody got tired of whittling on. The Ford Taurus was introduced in 1986 featuring "aerodynamic" styling—true, you couldn't actually cut yourself on the corners, but that was about it. See what you learn when you read?

Anyway, several movies have repeated this husband-gets-a-rude-awakening scenario, but *Mr. Mom* is the classic. At first he's pretty cocky about managing the home his way—how hard could it be? But as he burns meals, misplaces kids, wrecks the house, gets hooked on soap operas, gains weight, and more, he changes his tune. Eddie Murphy's 2003 movie *Daddy Daycare* has the same basic ignorant male theme with a similar ending: Pop learns new respect for how much work, organization, and leadership it takes to run a household and raise kids.

Thank God for movies, because I'd hate to learn this lesson firsthand. Besides, try to imagine paying someone to do the kind of things a stay-at-home wife does. You and I would have to work two jobs and maybe rob a liquor store on the way home. Though mercifully, most of us will never have to trade places, we may still have the temptation to critique our wives or to meddle with their systems at home (or at other places for that matter). Of course, there's plenty of opportunity for positive feedback if you have good communication skills. But imagine for a minute that you are Batman and you've brought a blindfolded guest into the high-tech domain of the Batcave. You remove the blindfold to reveal the wonders of what a billionaire can do with a secret, underground lair, and the first comments you hear are, "Who on earth picked out your colors? Is that mold I smell? Is it always so cold down here?" You know what I'd do if this happened to me? ***BAM! KAPOW! THWACK!*** Why should you expect to get a better reception from your wonder woman, especially when she's doing it all for you? The rule of the household should be: If it's hers to do, then it's mine to encourage.

If your wife works outside the home too, then your support can largely come from sharing the household chores and listening to *her* at the end of *her* long day. Swoop in to rescue her regularly. Even Catwoman wouldn't turn down a cup of coffee and a listening ear. Whatever your particular lifestyle, the tinkering a man likes to do should be saved for broken appliances.

Now for the perspective from the parallel universe where every superhero has his alter ego: some men do not meddle—they remove themselves entirely from the arena. Some men are perfectly happy to let their wives run the household, maybe even the whole show, without any comment, input, or criticism. Considering how strong some wonder women can be, it might be tempting to melt into *her* capable hands.

I knew one couple, both on their second marriage, who were a textbook example of this. He worked for her in her company, happily did whatever she told him to, and spent every spare moment on the golf course. (If you are a golfer, you may have to ignore this example.) Her comment one day to my wife said it all: "He's a good guy. Not too bright . . . but we're happy enough, I guess." She had all the authority at home, work, everywhere but the links—and that was what he lived for.

It's not that women shouldn't be strong or direct. I like direct people; it saves time guessing what they think. But the abandonment of your own leadership role because your wife is a force of nature is not a healthy response. God designed the wife to be fulfilled as a helper to her husband. Give her someone she's proud to assist. Even if she herself is a good leader, a woman who is married but not protected by her husband's leadership is insecure and frustrated in her vulnerability, even if she can't articulate its source. Step up and lead, even if you feel like you'd rather follow. And remember that if the household is her main arena, then don't confuse leadership with nitpicking.

**THE PROVERBS 31 HUSBAND DELEGATES
BUT DOES NOT ABDICATE.
AND WHEN HE DELEGATES, HE SUPPORTS WITH LOVE
AND IS NOT QUICK WITH CRITICISM.**

MOVING TESTIMONY

ANNE IS A DETERMINED DECORATOR, OR AS SHE LIKES TO DESCRIBE IT, ENVIRONMENTAL ENGINEER. Any number of times I have come home to our well-decorated abode to find it well *re*decorated. Not that she buys new stuff, but furniture I thought unmovable by human beings under six foot four casually graces different rooms . . . on different *floors*. One day I was particularly surprised to see the piano was not in its usual place and the TV armoire, which weighs more than a Hummer, was across the room.

"Why didn't you wait till I could help you?" I ask, trying to hide my glee over the fact that I didn't actually have to do anything (points for the willingness).

"It was no big deal. Kyle and Mom helped me."

At the time Kyle was nine, and Mom was seventy.

"Before you tell me the funeral arrangements, I'd love to know how you did it. I don't even see any blood."

"I worked a rug underneath the cabinet, and we slid it across the room."

"What about the piano?" Now I was sure she had to confess to being the *actual* Wonder Woman.

"Well, you know it has wheels."

I stared dumbly for a moment. *It does? You mean I could have rolled it when we moved in?!* Without letting on, I coolly responded, "I meant up that step from the den, yeah, from the den, I mean, of course, you could roll it from there. What about that step?"

"We managed." She smiled and changed the subject to how I liked it. Of course, I liked it fine; I liked it before too, but I wasn't about to help move it back. Funny how she can't open a mayonnaise jar when I'm available, but let me leave for work and nothing is too hard if it means she would otherwise have to wait to get it done!

HER HUSBAND IS
KNOWN IN THE GATES,
WHEN HE SITS AMONG
THE ELDERS OF THE LAND.

PROVERBS 31:23

TAKE PRIDE IN BEING KNOWN BY HER REPUTATION

PROVERBS 31:23 IS INTERESTING BECAUSE IT DOESN'T SAY WHY THE HUSBAND WAS KNOWN IN THE GATES; HE'S ONLY IDENTIFIED AS *HER* HUSBAND.

I understand what it's like to be *her* husband, since my wife has had a much higher profile than I have. She led worship at our church for almost three years, sings at conferences and coffeehouses, and has recorded her own CD. She gets letters from people she doesn't know and invitations to all kinds of places.

I get to keep the kids.

Sometimes the kids keep *me,* depending on whether or not they pool their forces. In the early years of our family, I tried to do theme nights. Ninja nights went over pretty well, and I managed to keep everyone alive, which, as I always pointed out to my wife, should count for something. Now our kids are older, and it's slightly harder keeping everyone alive, since I am more likely to follow through on threats to kill them. (After my wife's last conference, her accompanist's husband came running out to greet his wife *ahead* of their kids, waving his arms and shouting, "Mommy's home! Mommy's home!" So it's not just me.)

One time I had the kids at a restaurant, and a woman who had been watching us came up to the table and said, "Hi, I'm Vicky. You're Anne's husband, aren't you? I'm so sorry I don't know your name." I said, "I don't mind being known as 'Anne's husband,' and one day, if she hits it really big, I won't mind being known as 'Anne's *rich* husband' either."

I am always intrigued to learn about the spouses of famous people, especially of high-powered women. Sometimes it explains a lot, and sometimes it creates more questions. When I first saw former prime minister Margaret Thatcher's husband, Sir Denis, I remember being surprised. He wasn't what I had expected. But that was what piqued my curiosity. What on earth did a woman of her stature find appealing in him? Later as I researched about him, I discovered a truly admirable husband. He was a successful businessman who bankrolled her study of law as well as introduced her to many politically connected people. Of his high-profile wife he once said, **"For forty wonderful years I have been married to one of the greatest women the world has ever produced. All I could produce—small as it may be—was love and loyalty."** As for her opinion of him, she wrote in her autobiography, *The Downing Street Years,* "I could never have been prime minister for more than eleven years without Denis by my side. He was a fund of shrewd advice and penetrating comment. And he very sensibly saved these for me rather than the outside world." With his death in 2003, he was briefly the center of public attention outside the UK. Here is an excerpt from the news story that ran in the British newspaper the *Daily Telegraph:*

> Thatcher was a traditional husband, the master in his own house despite his wife's eminent role in the country. He had a rather old-fashioned view of the world, and in his marriage kept his male pursuits very much to himself. It was particularly remarkable, and a tribute to his enormous loyalty and integrity, that a man of Denis Thatcher's traditional outlook and generation could encourage his wife to shine.

From all accounts it was an honor for him to be known as "her husband."

I will concede that there's always the risk of this identity-by-association going too far. I suppose Sir Denis might have been annoyed by the occasional *Mr.* Margaret Thatcher comment, or the satire of him on British television. I suppose someone advised Robin that he'd do better as the Batboy. I suppose Major Steve Trevor sometimes lay awake at night thinking about marrying Wonder Woman and whether he could live as Wonder Man, or whether she would just hyphenate: Wonder Woman-Trevor.

No doubt about it, one's identity can be a sensitive subject. That's why I like the Fantastic Four. They never had *secret* identities. They were themselves—Reed Richards, Sue Storm, Johnny Storm, and Ben Grimm—but with nicknames because of their superpowers. That's not a bad idea for us *her* husbands to remember if we feel like we are losing our own identities. My true identity has never changed. I've just added a hero name for the sake of the admiring public: Her Husband! (Besides, with a quick touch-up it becomes Hero Husband!)

And that leads me to an interesting biblical principle. You put yourself at risk anytime you put your reputation into the hands of someone else. So imagine what God risks by allowing himself to be tied to individuals and their lives. He chose for centuries to be known as the God of Abraham, Isaac, and Jacob. Later, of Moses, David, Daniel, and even Samson! (Not to mention the nation of Israel.) Considering the outrageous things some of those guys did, it's particularly alarming that he'd let any of them be the custodian of his reputation. But as he wasn't asking my advice, God went ahead and sort of renamed himself, using their lives as part of his identity generation after generation. And that means he doesn't mind being known as the God of Jess MacCallum, or the God of *(your name)* either. Sort of makes you nervous for his sake, doesn't it? But if he makes himself vulnerable by being represented by me, then I suppose I can get used to being known by my wife's reputation. Besides, my status actually rises when I'm connected to her, which is more than God usually gets out of the deal with me.

THE PROVERBS 31 HUSBAND TAKES PRIDE IN HIS WIFE'S SHINING REPUTATION.

BIBLE QUIZ

MATCH THE WOMEN TO THEIR FAMOUS REPUTATIONS.

1. DEBORAH   4. HADASSAH

2. JAEL   5. RAHAB

3. RUTH   6. ABIGAIL

A. PRAISED IN SONG FOR HAMMERING A TENT PEG THROUGH THE SKULL OF THE CANAANITE ARMY'S COMMANDER WHILE HE SLEPT IN HER TENT. (JUDGES 4:21; 5:24)

B. PROSTITUTE WHO PROTECTED THE ISRAELITE SPIES IN JERICHO BY LYING TO THE KING, HIDING THEM ON HER ROOF, AND LETTING THEM DOWN THROUGH A WINDOW. (JOSHUA 2)

C. QUEEN OF PERSIA WHO FASTED THREE DAYS, RISKED HER LIFE, AND SAVED THE JEWISH NATION. (ESTHER 2:7)

D. SAVED HER ENTIRE HOUSEHOLD FROM DESTRUCTION BY HONORING DAVID, WHOM HER WICKED HUSBAND HAD INSULTED. (1 SAMUEL 25)

E. A PROPHETESS AND MOTHER WHO LED ISRAEL BECAUSE NO MAN WAS AS COMPETENT TO JUDGE. (JUDGES 4)

F. THE MOABITE WIDOW WHO GAVE UP EVERYTHING RATHER THAN LEAVE HER MOTHER-IN-LAW ALONE, ENDED UP MARRYING BOAZ, AND WAS INCLUDED IN THE LINEAGE OF CHRIST. (MATTHEW 1:5)

[1-E; 2-A; 3-F; 4-C; 5-B; 6-D]

STRENGTH AND DIGNITY ARE
HER CLOTHING,
AND SHE SMILES AT THE FUTURE.
SHE OPENS HER MOUTH IN WISDOM,
AND THE TEACHING OF KINDNESS
IS ON HER TONGUE.

PROVERBS 31:25, 26

UTILITY BELT ITEM #9

ACTUALLY LISTEN WHEN SHE SPEAKS

MOST MEN AREN'T GOOD LISTENERS. I have been a man too long not to notice. And even if I do forget this fact, my wonderful wife reminds me. I like to quote Homer Simpson on this point: "Just because I don't care doesn't mean I'm not listening." After enough years of marriage, this can be the most honest statement some men could make. We listen on autopilot; ears engaged, brain in neutral. It's the "yes, dear" nod. And sometimes it actually seems to be enough! She gets the attention she wants, and I don't get too worked up or involved. After all, haven't I been accused of trying to *fix* her problems instead of *just being there?* Doesn't she tell me she just wants me to let her talk it out? So what's the problem?

Apparently this kind of thinking comes from that two-hemispheres-of-the-brain syndrome I mentioned earlier. (The "don't involve me, but I'd do it this way" method.) I believe a whole-brain approach is needed. Even if men are fixers, the Proverbs 31 husband resists the urge to plunge straight in, tools in hand. At the same time, he gets involved in the process (however long it takes) of letting her talk things out. This really takes no superpower—unless, of course, she wants to talk during the play-offs.

But that's only phase one, when we learn to listen to her for *her* sake. We have to develop phase two listening—the listening we do for *our* sakes. Why not learn, as the Proverbs 31 husband did, that there's wisdom in her words? I have found—surprise of surprises—the more I listen, the more I learn! I can't count the ideas that I've gotten from listening to my wife. I frequently go to the office looking smarter than I was the day before. (Besides, I always appreciate being reminded my last name isn't Einstein when no one but her can see the look on my face.)

In 1 Samuel 25, there is a great example of a guy who had a Wonder Woman 31 but failed to value her wisdom. This rich, stupid husband was Nabal, and his wife's name was Abigail.

"And the woman was intelligent and beautiful in appearance, but the man was harsh and evil in his dealings" (verse 3). The story that follows is a great tale of how her wisdom saved her entire household.

During the time when David was roaming the countryside with his men—before he became king—he was forced to subsist as a sort of mercenary Captain America, er, Captain Israel. It was, however, an informal understanding, relying largely on the hospitality of the people he helped. A will-work-for-kosher arrangement. Here's where Nabal offended him. He had benefited from David's armed protection, but when David humbly asked for some consideration, Nabal blew him off as a runaway servant from a family of no account. Nabal's own servants knew better. They said David's men had been "like a wall of protection to us and the sheep" while they were shearing (verse 16, *NLT*). David's men had spent weeks protecting Nabal's interests only to be insulted by the man. David's take was clear: "A lot of good it did to help this fellow. We protected his flocks in the wilderness, and nothing he owned was lost or stolen. But he has repaid me evil for good" (verse 21, *NLT*). But his reaction wasn't exactly in keeping with the bylaws of the Justice League. "Get your swords!" (verse 13, *NLT*).

85

WHAT DID YOU SAY?

AFTER BEING AWAY FROM HOME ON A BUSINESS/FISHING TRIP, THE FIRST THING YOU WANT TO DO WHEN YOU GET HOME IS

A. listen to your wife talk about everything she, her friends, the kids, and the neighbors did while you were gone.

B. have sex.

C. enjoy a fine Scottish ale.

D. eat a steak while watching TV.

AFTER A LONG DAY OF PROBLEM SOLVING, WORKPLACE POLITICS, AND PERSONNEL MALFUNCTIONS, WHAT YOU WANT TO DO MOST WHEN YOU GET HOME IS

A. listen to your wife talk about her day in journalistic detail.

B. enjoy a fine Scottish ale.

C. eat a steak while watching TV.

D. have sex.

WHEN YOU ARE DONE WITH THE ENTIRE LIST OF CHORES THAT AVALANCHED YOUR OTHERWISE FREE SATURDAY—INCLUDING THINGS YOU COULD HAVE SWORN WERE STILL UNDECIDED—THE THING YOU MOST WANT TO DO IS

A. listen to your wife's assessment of your performance and her new list of things for next Saturday.

B. eat a steak while watching TV.

C. have sex.

D. enjoy a fine Scottish ale.

IF YOUR WIFE SAYS "WE NEVER TALK," THE RESPONSE YOU ARE MOST LIKELY TO GIVE IS: "WELL, HONEY, LET'S

A. talk."

B. have sex."

C. enjoy a fine Scottish ale."

D. eat a steak while watching TV."

IF YOU ANSWERED "A" TO ANY OF THE ABOVE, YOU CAN SKIP THIS CHAPTER. IN FACT YOU SHOULD PROBABLY BE *WRITING* THIS CHAPTER. YOU ARE THE ÜBERLISTENER. IF YOU ANSWERED WITH ANY OF THE OTHER LETTERS, TURN OFF THE TV AND READ THIS CHAPTER AGAIN.

And that might very well have been the end of Nabal's entire clan except for a certain mild-mannered housewife. Abigail's servants told her what had transpired, pleading for her help and explaining why they were approaching her, with one telling comment about Nabal—"He's so ill-tempered that no one can even talk to him!" (verse 17, *NLT*). Of course, they got no argument from Abigail; she had to put up with him day and night. She better than anyone knew he'd never listen.

So as superheroes always do, she sprang into action! She packed up enough food and wine to make David's 600 men happy—that's a lot of Chianti—and headed out with her servants to meet David, "but she didn't tell her husband what she was doing" (verse 19, *NLT*). Upon meeting David's band, she threw herself in between him and her household, and appeased his anger by her words. David, who always had an eye for the ladies, was impressed. He blurted out, **"Praise the Lord, the God of Israel, who has sent you to meet me today! Thank God for your good sense! Bless you for keeping me from murdering the man and carrying out vengeance with my own hands"** (verses 32, 33, *NLT*). After receiving her gifts, he showed the distinguishing feature of a man who appreciated a Proverbs 31 woman: "Go up to your house in peace. **See, I have *listened* to you and granted your request"** (verse 35). David clearly saw the wisdom in her appeal to avoid revenge. Abigail had not only rescued her household, she had rescued David from making a big mistake.

Now here's the ironic part of the story.

When Abigail arrived home, she found that Nabal had thrown a big party and was celebrating like a king. He was very drunk, so she didn't tell him anything about her meeting with David. The next morning when he was sober, she told him what had happened. He had a stroke, and he lay on his bed paralyzed. "About ten days later, the Lord struck Nabal and he died" (verse 38, *NLT*).

Nabal finally listened to his wife! When David was told Nabal had died, he praised God that he hadn't followed through on his plans to slaughter Nabal's household, and being no fool, immediately proposed to Abigail. Now there's an interesting how-Mommy-and-Daddy-met story for the kids.

Had Nabal survived his foolishness, he would have deserved the biggest—and I do mean the biggest—"I told you so." Not that he would have listened even then. Hopefully, we will not need to learn from a wifely "I told you so." It's better than being slaughtered by angry Israelites, of course, but just slightly.

Sometimes the wisdom our amazing wives come up with may be buried under a lot of other information we'd rather not sort through. At other times their observations are just so simple, it's too embarrassing to admit we didn't come up with them first. The fact is, women simply interpret things and draw conclusions in ways that would never occur to men. All that "women's intuition" stuff seems truer the longer I am married. It's apparently a superpower that is largely incompatible with the Y chromosome we men possess. **God designed the wife to be a "helper suitable" to the man (Genesis 2:18).** Her purpose is to complete me. By really listening I extend the chance for her to exercise that role, and I have the chance to see with a sort of borrowed X-ray vision. What rational reason could I have for missing that opportunity?

THE PROVERBS 31 HUSBAND LEARNS TO LISTEN TO HIS WIFE'S WORDS AND SEEKS HER THOUGHTS TO HELP OPEN HIS EYES.

HER **CHILDREN RISE UP** AND
BLESS HER;
HER HUSBAND ALSO,
AND HE **PRAISES HER,** SAYING:
"MANY DAUGHTERS HAVE DONE NOBLY,
BUT YOU **EXCEL** THEM ALL."

PROVERBS 31:28, 29

<table>
<tr><td>UTILITY
BELT
ITEM
◇#10◇</td><td>PRAISE HER AND TEACH YOUR CHILDREN TO PRAISE HER</td></tr>
</table>

MOST OF US HAVE DAYDREAMED ABOUT BEING BORN WITH SUPERPOWERS. As a kid I used to tie a towel around my neck and jump from the bookshelves onto a pile of sofa cushions. When we bought a new appliance I had "concrete" (Styrofoam) blocks to break with my bare fists. Nerf guns proved I had a chest of steel. I even remember contemplating whether I would let a spider bite me if there were *any* chance of ending up like Spider-Man. I never had the nerve to follow through on that one. But inheriting a ring of power or being granted telepathic powers from a painless alien visit would have been equally nice. Training incessantly like Batman held absolutely no interest. If it came easily and made me powerful, then I was up for it. Unfortunately, that disposition has stuck with me into adulthood, while superpowers never showed up.

So when it comes to this particular passage (Proverbs 31:28, 29) describing the Proverbs 31 husband, I have to take a deep breath, and it's not because the towel I tied around my neck is too tight. It's because I have to do something that I am not naturally super at.

The last thing that comes naturally to me is the language of praise. It's been like learning Mandarin Chinese. (Of course, for one-fifth of the world, that's no big deal. I guess people in China say something is as hard as learning Italian; and the Italians probably say something's as hard as building a reliable car.) Sarcasm is my native tongue, with a crisp, critical accent. But criticism is the privilege of the judge and not the servant. God has taught me a lot about watching my mouth, but for some reason I still need daily reminders. Even in my compliments I've had to learn to be careful. "Wow, this place looks great—thought I was in the wrong house for a minute" or "Sure, I'd love to take you out to dinner, honey—in fact if I could afford it, you'd never cook again" or "You look great in that outfit—not many women your age could wear that" or "You haven't gained weight—maybe added a bit of insulation." So at the risk of inventing a really sappy metaphor—praise and exhortation are like equal parts rain and sunshine; criticism is only a harsh wind that tears down to the roots. We need to create an environment of praise to create an environment of growth. (OK, there it is; no more Hallmark moments.)

If our wives are praiseworthy, then we need to take note of every opportunity to praise them. Daily. Period. Whether it comes naturally or not. God made us initiators *and* servants in our marriages. Is there a better place to start than building our wives up with praise? Even if, as in my case, it isn't the thing that earned you a cape and a letter on your chest. It's a power nonetheless. Just open your mouth and let some praise for your superwife come out. If you can't think of anything one day, just repeat yesterday's. If you have to, make something up. In fact, according to this verse, we have the right to compare our wives to others. So now you have plenty of material! (Normally I adhere to that standard *Sesame Street* stuff about everyone being special in his own way, but this verse allows me one opportunity to blow that off.) Praising her by a favorable comparison reinforces her singularity. It affirms your wife's superiority in your eyes consistent with your wedding vows, "forsaking all others." It puts the wonder back in Wonder Woman! Choose some celebrity, for example, and tell your wife she's more talented than her. Tell her she's better in some way than each one of her friends.

BECOME A **SUPER FAMILY**

- HAVE YOUR KIDS DRAW A PICTURE OF THEIR SUPERMOM IN THEIR FAVORITE SUPERCOSTUME.

- WRITE A THEME SONG FOR YOUR WONDER WOMAN AND TEACH IT TO THE KIDS TO SING TO HER WHEN SHE'S WORN OUT.

- MAKE MOTHER'S DAY A MONTHLY EVENT. YOU AND THE KIDS PLAN HOW TO MAKE THE SECOND SUNDAY OF *EVERY* MONTH SPECIAL FOR MOM.

- WHENEVER YOU GO BY THE STORE (AND YOU *SHOULD* BE GOING TO THE STORE), BUY YOUR AMAZING SPOUSE HER "KEY TO THE CITY": HER FAVORITE CANDY, A MAGAZINE, OR THE OLD STANDBY—FLOWERS. SOMETHING FOR YOU AND THE KIDS TO SHOW YOUR APPRECIATION.

- TAKE FIFTEEN MINUTES AND BRAINSTORM ALL THE LITTLE THINGS YOU CAN PRAISE YOUR WIFE FOR. WRITE THEM DOWN. KEEP THEM BESIDE YOUR COMPUTER AT WORK AND E-MAIL ONE TO YOUR DYNAMIC BETTER HALF ONE OR TWO TIMES A WEEK. IF YOUR KIDS ARE INTO TECHNOLOGY, LET THEM TEXT-MESSAGE HER THE SAME WAY.

The trick here is not to run down the other woman—that would defeat the purpose. It should be someone who has "done nobly." Tell your wife she's more determined than Batgirl, tougher than Supergirl, thinner than Sue Storm. Now *that* would mean something to her.

Of course, if all else fails pick a stranger at random. At a restaurant once I pointed to a woman I didn't even know and said, "See that woman? You're far smarter than she is."

"How do *you* know?" asked my wife.

"Because she's not married to *me*."

Just begin somewhere. It's essential that we practice this because even though it begins with us, it's not supposed to stop there. If, or when, you have children, they are supposed to be praising their supermom along with you. The great part is that most kids have a natural sense of wonder about their parents. For example, my daughters think I am the handsomest man who ever walked the earth. (Someday, of course, they will discover that this is only partly true—they really can't know about the ones who are already dead. So for now I am the handsomest man *alive.* I can live with that.) It's very flattering how our kids tend to view us. To them, we *really are* superheroes. We are stronger and faster than them, and we regularly rescue them from everything from bad dreams to splinters, from itchy backs to high fevers. But we have to remember that their natural awe of Marvelous Mom can be either encouraged or dulled by what they hear Dynamic Dad say. I remember the first time I heard my own caustic tone come out of my son's mouth. He was about three. For a couple of years, I thought he'd grow out of it. Then I realized that since *I* hadn't yet, I should address the problem. Teach your children by changing how you speak to their blessed mother. Don't let them have to learn Mandarin Chinese later in life.

THE PROVERBS 31 HUSBAND REGULARLY PRAISES HIS WIFE AND HELPS HIS CHILDREN DO THE SAME.

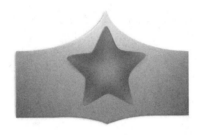

CHARM IS DECEITFUL AND
BEAUTY IS VAIN,
BUT A WOMAN WHO
FEARS THE LORD,
SHE SHALL BE PRAISED.

PROVERBS 31:30

UTILITY
BELT
ITEM
#11

FOCUS ON **WHAT GOD** **FINDS ATTRACTIVE** **AND PRAISEWORTHY**

WHEN IT COMES TO BEING DISTRACTED BY ATTRACTIVE WOMEN AND CHARMED BY WITTY FEMININE CONVERSATION, I MUST CONFESS THAT I AM THE CLASSIC PUSHOVER. There is a "kryptonite effect" I read about in an exercise magazine at the gym one day when I should have been, in fact, exercising. Apparently, science has once again confirmed what we already knew about ourselves from junior high—beautiful girls make us stupid, frequently robbing us of the power of speech, eye control, and financial judgment (a fact that the Hooters restaurant chain has parlayed into a multimillion-dollar business and an *airline* of all things!). You've got to wonder if part of Wonder Woman's power wasn't the distraction factor of a knockout in a strapless one-piece and go-go boots!

I have experienced sitcom-type moments where I have actually stumbled over my own name. It was more frequent when I was younger, but it is far more embarrassing now that I'm in my forties. I should be well past that adolescent thinking, right? But I still get a funny, awkward, boyish feeling if a good-looking woman pays a little attention to me.

I certainly was mush-mouthed when I met my wife—but at least I had an excuse: we were both fifteen years old (a bit of historical data I am actively trying to hide from my teen and preteen children). When I first saw her, I was flattened. I did my best to stare *casually.* But there is something the Proverbs 31 husband has learned about beauty and charm that hormones, and our culture, argue against. They aren't to be trusted.

Feminine beauty is a particularly wobbly concept when you think about it. It changes from year to year, culture to culture, and magazine cover to magazine cover. All it takes to establish the shifting nature of physical beauty is a quick look through an art history textbook. Botticelli's *Venus?* The *Mona Lisa?* Yikes! Takes all the interest out of time travel for me, personally. But from a sociological standpoint, no people group anywhere or anytime has been without a standard of womanly beauty, even if no one else gets it. Sort of like the 1970s.

And the list of absurd things people will do to get, or keep, beauty is truly endless. From ancient Japanese women grinding iron filings into their teeth to create a gorgeous black smile, to Victorian ladies in corsets that literally squeezed their internal organs into an hourglass figure, to Hollywood has-beens with more face-lifts than ex-husbands—beauty has ruled the senseless. And men have prized it above reason and valued it entirely out of proportion. Seventeenth-century French philosopher Blaise Pascal points out this absurdity in his *Pensées*: "The nose of Cleopatra, if it had been shorter, would have changed the whole face of the earth."

Does that mean, or does Proverbs 31:30 imply, that outward beauty is a *bad* thing? No, just not something one should be basing decisions on. By nature it is fleeting, elusive, and unconnected to true virtue. Beauty frequently distracts from things we should be examining and promises things it can't fulfill. **Proverbs 27:20 says that in man's natural state his eyes are never satisfied.**

This can create quite a tension in those of us who want to be like the husband of Wonder Woman 31. If outward appearance is disproportionate in my reckoning of value, I will create a downward spiral of dissatisfaction for myself, and frustration for my wife. We see it every day in the entertainment world. "Hunky actor trades jaw-dropping starlet for new companion." Think about it. If beauty alone could do it, Jessica Simpson and what's-his-face would have been the happiest couple in the world, not last year's tabloid headlines.

Now let me state the obvious. Of course we are supposed to find our spouses attractive. My wife wants to be attractive to me. She spends time taking care of herself, buys flattering clothes, and bathes at least once a month whether she needs it or not. It's the way women are wired. I saw a classic snapshot of this one afternoon. I was grabbing a quick lunch alone at a Hardee's near my office, watching the crowd come and go, thinking about work stuff. In the middle of my 7,000-calorie combo, a woman walked in. Late fifties, easily over six feet, and "big-boned" I guess would be the polite thing to say. ("Big-boned" as in a display at the Smithsonian.) She was wearing something in between a warm-up suit and a tent. But the thing that really caught my eye was the crown of barrel-sized curlers in her hair. No scarf, no hat, just curlers wrapped with impossibly black hair, for a woman her age. She strode up to the counter, ordered a meal, stood casually while they filled her order, and then left. Apparently, she was totally unconcerned with her appearance. *Man,* I thought, *imagine being seen in public like that.* (I never claimed to be mature.) Then I was struck by a competing thought: she was getting ready to look good for someone, and it wasn't any of us! There was only one man on her mind, and it was his staring she cared about. Someone was going to see her at her best that night, and the rest didn't matter. Now that's my kind of gal!

My own wife loves to hear me say she's beautiful, and she really is, so that makes it easy for me, Shallow Man. There's plenty of Scripture to support the idea of finding your wife beautiful. But what the husband in Proverbs 31 has apparently learned is that while the world incessantly praises beauty, in the eternal picture it doesn't count for much. It is what it is, and it ain't what it ain't. And it ain't as praiseworthy as a woman who fears the Lord is.

Besides, it cuts both ways. Shouldn't I be relieved that I am not held to the impossible standard of perpetual handsomeness? I certainly can't guarantee how much longer I'm going to keep my above-average good looks. I might not even age with rugged, masculine appeal, although that's more or less my current plan (Sean Connery style). But if both of us could grow that inner attractiveness even as the outer is changing its form, then we both have a lifetime of beauty to look forward to. The Proverbs 31 husband has a proper perspective on the value of inner versus outer beauty.

If beauty isn't to be overvalued, the Proverbs 31 husband knows that charm is outright bogus. Think about it. The dialogue for supervillains is *always* better than for superheroes. It's wittier, cooler, and far more quotable. But it is still said by the bad guys.

It's for good reason that **Proverbs 7:21 (*NLT*) says, "So she seduced him with her pretty speech and enticed him with her flattery."** Charm is the same thing as flattery, and the beginning of trouble. It's a cliché to call someone who knows how to get what they want with flattery a "charmer." Even the word has a questionable past. Charms are spells that are intended to bring good fortune—in other words, to get what you want out of life by magic. And, as Ellen DeGeneres has proven, beauty and charm don't always come as a package. Charm does not require beauty; it can act alone. Whereas beauty is focused primarily on the object (a stunning blonde secretary), charm is focused on the subject (the gullible office manager). The more unprepared you are, the easier it is for the tractor beam of deception to carry you away. It's surely easy to fall for charming people. Look at some of the people we've elected to high offices!

In utter contrast to these two flashy attention-getters, the "fear of the Lord" is the true basis for praise. It's a healthy, awed respect, with a Superman-ish commitment to Truth (2 Corinthians 13:8), Justice (Isaiah 30:18), and the . . . well, just the Way (John 14:6). This fear of the Lord is the beginning of knowledge and wisdom (Proverbs 1:7; 9:10), prolongs life (10:27), provides shelter (14:26), and is rewarded by riches, honor, and life (22:4). Now that's more than enough reason to choose fear of the Lord over beauty and charm in a wife! If we practice it ourselves, we will encourage it in our mates. No marriage could be more superhuman than one built mutually on the fear of the Lord.

Let me add one serious warning: many men allow their marriages to be ended by the undeniable double whammy of beauty and charm in another woman. If you don't think you are vulnerable, remember Batman and Catwoman? or Poison Ivy? Batman almost bought the farm with both of them. Beware! No would-be hero is overconfident in the face of the archenemy, or his traps.

> **THE PROVERBS 31 HUSBAND KNOWS WHAT REAL BEAUTY IS AND AVOIDS BEING DUPED BY CHARM. HE KNOWS THAT THE LOOKS, OR LIPS, OF ANOTHER WOMAN COULD SPELL THE DEATH OF HIS MARRIAGE!**

MY TOP TEN FAVORITE
QUOTES ON BEAUTY

WHAT A STRANGE ILLUSION IT IS TO SUPPOSE THAT BEAUTY IS GOODNESS.
~Leo Tolstoy, Russian writer and philosopher

THERE IS A ROAD FROM THE EYE TO THE HEART THAT DOES NOT GO THROUGH THE INTELLECT.
~G. K. Chesterton, English writer and Christian apologist

MY WORK ALWAYS TRIED TO UNITE THE TRUTH WITH THE BEAUTIFUL, BUT WHEN I HAD TO CHOOSE ONE OR THE OTHER, I USUALLY CHOSE THE BEAUTIFUL.
~Hermann Weyl, German mathematician and physicist

BEAUTY IS INDEED A GOOD GIFT OF GOD; BUT THAT THE GOOD MAY NOT THINK IT A GREAT GOOD, GOD DISPENSES IT EVEN TO THE WICKED.
~Augustine of Hippo, fourth- and fifth-century bishop and theologian

BEAUTY IS A SHORT-LIVED TYRANNY.
~Socrates, ancient Greek philosopher

THERE'S A DIFFERENCE BETWEEN BEAUTY AND CHARM. A BEAUTIFUL WOMAN IS ONE I NOTICE. A CHARMING WOMAN IS ONE WHO NOTICES ME.
~John Erskine, American essayist and educator

BEAUTY STANDS IN THE ADMIRATION ONLY OF WEAK MINDS LED CAPTIVE.
~John Milton, seventeenth-century English poet

A THING OF BEAUTY IS A JOB FOREVER.
~Milton Berle, American comedian and actor

EVEN I DON'T WAKE UP LOOKING LIKE CINDY CRAWFORD.
~Cindy Crawford, American supermodel

THE AVERAGE GIRL WOULD RATHER HAVE BEAUTY THAN BRAINS BECAUSE SHE KNOWS THE AVERAGE MAN CAN SEE BETTER THAN HE CAN THINK.
~Anonymous

MY ONE **FAVORITE QUOTE** ON **CHARM**

YOU KNOW WHAT CHARM IS: A WAY OF GETTING THE ANSWER YES WITHOUT HAVING ASKED ANY CLEAR QUESTION.
~Albert Camus, French author and philosopher

GIVE HER THE PRODUCT
OF HER HANDS,
AND LET HER WORKS PRAISE
HER IN THE GATES.

PROVERBS 31:31

<table>
<tr><td>UTILITY
BELT
ITEM
◆#12◆</td><td>## BRAG ABOUT HER
IN PUBLIC</td></tr>
</table>

WE MEN LOVE TO BE ACKNOWLEDGED FOR OUR ACCOMPLISHMENTS. From being featured on the cover of the company newsletter to having the mayor of Metropolis present you with the key to the city, it feels great. If I fix a leaky faucet, I want a news release about it. Maybe for that reason I identify so easily with the characters from the 1999 movie *Mystery Men*. Without a doubt one of my favorite movies, it chronicles would-be superheroes as they try to break into the business. But with superpowers like shoveling, throwing forks, and a really bad temper, they just can't quite seem to capture the attention of the media. Like those guys, I want some credit even if I fall short of the mark.

113

Just before we brought our first baby home from the hospital, I launched into a major cleanup project to "help" my wife (and maybe earn a little mileage with my mother-in-law). The fact that I chose to clean up my own files and my own papers in my own desk seemed like a good idea to me, but somehow it didn't have the impact on my wife that I expected. She didn't even thank me!

To grossly oversimplify (one of my special powers), recognition is tied to men's sense of purpose and to women's sense of identity. Adam's role was established as a doer even before Eve came along (tending the garden, naming the animals, hanging out with God). But he was incomplete by design; **his aloneness was the only thing pronounced "not good" (Genesis 2:18).** Eve's role was to complete Adam; it was her identity to make him whole so together they could fulfill God's ultimate purpose beyond the Garden of Eden—to have sex (no, really), raise enough children to invent SEC basketball, and then run everything. (I am not making this up—see Genesis 1:28.)

In light of this superheroic task, it's easy to see how receiving praise for the things we accomplish strikes each of us down to

TOP TWELVE LIST

OF THE THREE WORDS
A WOMAN WANTS TO HEAR

(AFTER "I LOVE YOU")

1. YOU WERE RIGHT.
2. I WAS WRONG.
3. I AM SORRY.
4. LET'S EAT OUT.
5. YOU LOOK THINNER.
6. I'LL CLEAN UP.
7. LET'S JUST CUDDLE.
8. CAN I VACUUM?
9. YOUR MOTHER'S WELCOME.
10. WHICH CHORE FIRST?
11. TAKE YOUR TIME.
12. BUY THEM BOTH.

the roots of our own unique designs. And since our task is a worldwide assignment, why shouldn't public recognition be appropriate? See where the acknowledgment of the woman's outstanding behavior occurs in Proverbs 31:31 above? It's at the city gates—where no one can miss it.

I should probably add a word of balance here for the sake of any Captain Amazing with his spandex too tight. **We are not encouraging our wives to do their good deeds "before men to be noticed by them" (Matthew 6:1).** Jesus had a warning for folks like that: "you have no reward with your Father who is in heaven" (Matthew 6:1). But that applies to our *own* motivation. It in no way stops us from publicizing the good deeds of other people. If your wonder woman is doing great things, find those city gates and start blabbing!

And speaking of blabbing, I have learned an interesting lesson about my words—any comment I make is amplified in a public setting. A little praise becomes a huge encouragement, and a teasing joke can feel like a stab in the back. I learned this the hard way (about the only way I learn). It took a few silent rides home from dinner parties before I caught on. *Clearly,* I thought,

she can't take a joke; I was just being clever, even charming!
Tease her about stuff at home, no problem; tease her in front of
others, and just feel the burning gaze of her heat-ray vision!

So why do even well-intentioned Christian husbands continue
to make this mistake? Because in our culture there are two
people that account for 50 percent of all jokes that men tell:
the wife and the mother-in-law. (Even women make jokes about
their mothers-in-law.) Ever since Henny Youngman (the post-
Vaudeville stand-up comic who came up with the infamous one-
liner, "Take my wife, please!"), it's been open season on the ones
we are supposed to take care of. It's become so ingrained in our
thinking that sometimes a jab at "the old ball-and-chain" just
pops out of our mouths in front of other people.

But let me tell you, switch from making your wife the brunt of
the joke to putting her on a pedestal in public, and those long,
silent rides home will be transformed into romantic journeys!
(Remember, never make fun of someone you are hoping
to "be fruitful and multiply" with.) Praising your wife for her
accomplishments in front of others is one of the quickest ways to
transform your marriage.

Years ago I took my wife to a meeting of a national association of the public relations industry. At that time I was still active in the sales side of our business as the vice president of sales and marketing. As usual, to provide networking opportunities, the people at each table were asked to stand up and introduce themselves and their guests. It quickly became clear to me that virtually everyone in the room, including myself, had a title— except my wife, who was a stay-at-home mom for our first two kids. When it was my turn, I introduced myself, and then my wife: "This is my wife, Anne. She's Director of Human Resources and the Vice President of Environmental Control for two preschoolers. She's responsible for everything from basic hygiene and language acquisition to social integration and emotional well-being." The room burst into applause, all those potential clients remembered who I was—especially the women—and Anne felt like a million bucks. (Plus I had one of those great rides home.)

Assuming you have made it this far into the book and are not just browsing around at a newsstand waiting for your flight, you must have a dynamic wife too. If so, I have a suggestion for you: start a fan club for your wonder woman. If you think she's amazing, I bet others will as well. My wife is a songwriter and vocalist, and I am truly her biggest fan. Fortunately, she's really good—fortunate because I'd still have to be her biggest fan even if she weren't. It doesn't have to be an official fan club of course, with decoder rings and a secret handshake. It can be sort of off the record. It's not that hard. First, make yourself the unofficial president. Second, bring her up as a topic among friends and coworkers. Tell about her amazing feats of womanhood, her astounding skills, and her selfless devotion to mankind (meaning you primarily). Whenever you can, demonstrate the admiration a club member should have. Do not let un-fanlike comments or attitudes go uncorrected! Step three, seek unofficial associate members: the dog, the in-laws, the neighbors, strangers.

Consider one other issue on this point. Not only is public recognition great for your wife and great for your marriage, it's great for you too. The image I project of my wife to others becomes a two-sided billboard with a picture of her on the front and me on the back. Ever known a guy who finds only his wife's failings suitable for discussion? While he's painting a hideous portrait of her, you can't help but think this guy must be a royal loser! How could he let his marriage get so bad? If he's right about her, how could anyone be stupid enough to marry someone so monstrous? And then broadcast it to the world! If I were that clueless, I'd at least keep my mouth shut. Now consider the opposite scenario. Imagine there's a new guy at work who's done nothing but sing his wife's praises for the six months he's been there. Every time he gets the chance, he says how great she is, or how smart, or how talented, or that she rescued a baby from a burning building last night. When you finally get to meet her, it will be like meeting a celebrity! To paraphrase the old Vidal Sassoon shampoo commercial: If *you* don't look good, *I* don't look good. Really, if you convince people your wife is *the* Wonder Woman, can they really help but think you're Superman?

**THE PROVERBS 31 HUSBAND RECOGNIZES HIS WIFE'S ACCOMPLISHMENTS AND BROADCASTS HIS ADMIRATION OF HER TO THE WORLD.
NO ONE WONDERS WHAT HE THINKS OF HER—
HE FREELY SHARES HIS OPINIONS.**

CONCLUSION

I never would have imagined the adventure I was undertaking when I married my Wonder Woman 31. I knew she was unique, but I am still learning just how amazing she is. And that's the great thing really—witnessing a strong, capable woman apply her gifts to become the Proverbs 31 wife God called her to be. Any man who marries a Christian woman, by definition, marries the daughter of the King. But some of us have been hitched up to Diana the Amazon Princess! I sincerely hope that these thoughts have both entertained and stimulated you to take pride in your wife's strengths, to not be threatened by her God-given characteristics, and to thank God for not letting you go through life unscrubbed and unpolished. The world needs strong wives to build strong families. Just remember you are still to be the Super Man-of-the-House, even if she's flying higher, moving faster, or leaping taller department stores (and then stopping in to see what's on sale).

Enjoy the ride. And if you have sons, they'll get the right idea from chapter after chapter of their own in-house Captain Amazing. And if you are lucky enough to have a daughter, maybe she'll be the next Supergirl for some unsuspecting Boy Wonder. Then you can swing into action to mentor him, Caped Crusader!

By the way, when you read the Bible from now on, watch out for these Wonder Women 31. They pop up here and there, sometimes very quietly. In fact, Proverbs 31 itself isn't just *about* these heroines. It was formed by one. Proverbs 31:1—"The words of King Lemuel, the oracle which his mother taught him."

FOREWORD BY SHAUNTI FELDHAHN

THAT CRAZY
LITTLE THING CALLED
LOVE
THE SOUNDTRACK OF MARRIAGE, SEX, AND FAITH
JUD WILHITE

Love has a way of making people sing. Songs like "I Only Have Eyes for You," "Stand by Your Man," "Love Me Tender," and "Livin' on a Prayer" come to mind. Yet three thousand years ago, a king of Israel wrote a love song—the Song of Solomon—filled with passionate and insightful principles for relationships that were true then . . . and now.

That Crazy Little Thing Called Love
ISBN 10: 0-7847-1944-6   ISBN 13: 978-0-7847-1944-2